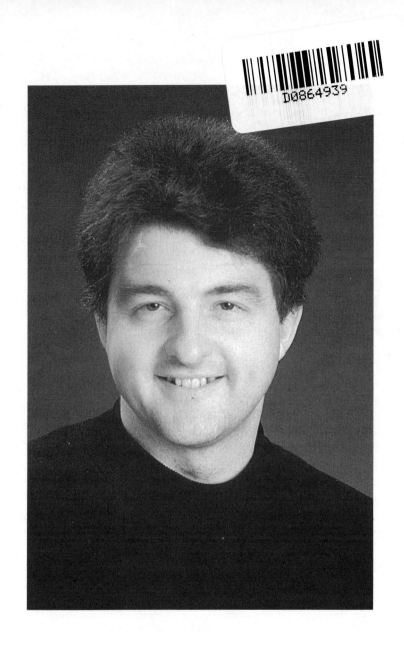

The Waistband
and other poems

The Waistband
and other poems

Donny O'Rourke

Polygon
Edinburgh

© Donny O'Rourke 1997

Published by Polygon
22 George Square
Edinburgh

Set in Bembo by Hewer Text Composition Services, Edinburgh
Printed and bound in Great Britain by
The Cromwell Press

A CIP record is available

ISBN 0 7486 6232 4

The Publisher acknowledges subsidy from

THE SCOTTISH ARTS COUNCIL

towards the publication of this volume.

For Dan and Hester's children,
Stephen and Maureen
and their children

'Not to find one's way about in a city is of little interest . . . but to lose one's way in a city, as one loses one's way in a forest, requires practice.'

Walter Benjamin

'They sentenced me to thirty years of boredom for trying to change the system from within.'

Leonard Cohen, *First We Take Manhattan*

'Sincerity is the one great artistic crime. Insincerity is the second greatest.'

Fernando Pessoa, *On Sensationism*

'Of course true love is exceptional, two or three times a century more or less. The rest of the time there is vanity or boredom.'

Abert Camus, *The Fall*

The heart is a resilient little muscle.

Woody Allen

CONTENTS

ACKNOWLEDGEMENTS

Acknowledgements are due to the editors of the following publications in which several of these poems (or versions of them) first appeared: *Cambridge Yearbook of Comparative Literature*, *Cencrastus*, *Chapman*, *The Dark Horse*, *Edinburgh Review*, *Fuente*, *Gairfish*, *The (Glasgow) Herald*, *Lines Review*, *New Writing Scotland*, *Paper Cuts*, *Radical Scotland*, *The Scotsman*, *Skinklin' Star*, *South-fields*, *Verse* and *West Coast Magazine*. Poems were printed in the following anthologies: *A Scottish Feast* and *Mungo's Tongues* and in the text books *Ways of Reading* and *Working Words*. Others were broadcast on Radio Clyde, Radio Forth, Radio Tay, Radio 3, Radio 5, Radio Scotland, RTE, WFMT Chicago, Sverige Radio 1 and Scottish Television. This collection reprints work from the Vennel pamphlet *Second Cities*, and contains selections from *Eftirs/Afters* (Au Quai Press) and *On Your Nerve: A Wake for Frank O'Hara* (Verse Magazine), a performance piece devised and staged by W. N. Herbert, David Kinloch and Donny O'Rourke which was premiered at the CCA, Glasgow, during Mayfest 1997. Dave Whyte performed *Still Waiting to be Wise* for the first time at the same festival. A Fellowship awarded by the Scottish Arts Council and the Universities of Glasgow and Strathclyde bought the time some of these poems and songs needed. The students were a delight. At the Glasgow School of Art I found inspiring people in an inspiring building. For almost a decade Ann Karkalas in the Department of Adult and Continuing Education at Glasgow University has been an exemplary colleague and patient friend. Thanks respectively to Peter McCaughey and Krista Mits I got to read (and write) in Porto and Tallinn. For excellent advice from marvellous poets, I thank James Aitchison and Philip Hobsbaum.

A short stay in Geneva at La Maison McCarey and a long one with Bill Currie in Chicago offered respite and stimulus in exactly the right proportions. I'm reminded on every page of Richard, David and Robin whom I thank for their friendship and support.

The prose memoir with which the book begins was commissioned by the *Scotsman* newspaper. Pieces printed in italics are song lyrics, the fruits of a hugely enjoyable partnership with Dave Whyte.

Thanks finally to John Hawthorn and all my teachers without whom . . .

Growing up on the lower Clyde
Argyll was greener on the other side
We watched the last Cunarder glide
        Down to the sea.

I'm not nostalgic for other men's sweat
There's plenty about the old days we should forget
But Clyde built boats could be sailing yet
        Down to the sea.

Listen to the voices of skilled tradesmen
Sold down their own river for 30 yen
But you don't need ships to sail again
        Down to the sea.

Every apprentice that learned a trade
Every ship they ever made
Those are ghosts that wont be laid
(They sail)   Down to the sea.

Greenock's reason was its river and that's still so
Though all it does these days is flow
In welder's dreams tugs still go
        Down to the sea.

My father's eyes were boiler-suit blue
He took pride in what he'd learned to do
Now no-one needs the craft he knew
(To go)   Down to the sea.

Growing up on the lower Clyde
Argyll was greener on the other side
We watched the last Cunarder glide
        Down to the sea.

Down to the sea, down to the sea
We watched the last Cunarder glide
        Down to the sea.

FOREWORD: Port of Recall

Born 1959 in Port Glasgow. There and then it's true; but when I see it stated in a publisher's blurb or conference press release, the facts are never cold. I left Port Glasgow in my mother's arms, so this journey's a sentimental one – short and bitter-sweet: a ghost train ride to a town that never was. Yet the only town for me.

Time travellers need their fetishes and jujus. Preparations must be made. By my bed, I keep my father's missal, miniature, maroon, its pages gilt-edged, guilt-dredged. Obsolete as hell. A gorgeous ribbon minds his place: Dan O'Rourke, 1 Huntly Place, Port Glasgow. His exquisite slate-perfected copperplate, hardly faded.

Then there's the photograph: a blurry sepia 10 × 8, quietly angling for attention on the pine kist in my living room: 63 men (each one counted), 60 assorted cloth caps, two bare heads, one bowler. Between the foreman's knees, a chalked on blackboard: 'John G. Kincaid & Co Ltd, Turning Shop (Arthur Street), 7.5.30'. The youth in the Bowery Boy bunnet kneeling in the bottom left hand corner, the one who's pouting, will wait nearly thirty years before becoming my dad. Now he's twenty, his time newly 'out', an engineer in the engineering capital of the world. Underneath that cap there bristles the fullest head of hair in Port Glasgow. The Depression is about to begin.

Lastly, for luck, another picture. This one's a painting. I wish it were mine but it's a short walk away across the park in Kelvingrove Art Gallery: Stanley Spencer's *The Glen: Port Glasgow* – a bacchanal, a crucifixion, the wide world turning its wilkies, when a boy in a Fair Isle jumper dreeps from the railings of the street Dan lived in long ago with his six sisters, three brothers and the memory of Billy lost to infant mortality. This talisman I cannot touch; it touches me.

Getting there's easy. Since 1841, thanks to the Caledonian Railway Company, rails have raced the river all the way, joined these days by the M8. I pay for an away day ticket, £3.60 for a happy return, except I'm not.

This is the line that runs right through my life, a couple of years in London notwithstanding. Writing Fellow at my *alma mater*, the BBC, STV, the BEEB again: break out, or break down.

The sprinter reels on, puffed out by Paisley where I went to schools that no longer exist. Sacred Heart's been bypassed. 'The Academy', (*aka* St Mirin's), is a technical college annexe. An ex-pupil is John Byrne. Another's Gerry Rafferty – from Renfrew Road to *Reservoir Dogs*, an ear for a tune all right, the boy.

But Bishopton, sunny Bishopton: compost for growing kids, woods and water, the Royal Ordnance factory where dad worked for forty years at a lathe and few do now. The Scouts (the 1st Bishopton, 66th Renfrewshire), hiking, biking, a nice green nowhere with a pretty graveyard and six trains an hour. And we're away: on to Langbank – a nicey nice highish-price, cosy, dormitory of a place. A motorway runs through it. And so does this train. Just after Bishopton, the river winks broadly into view at what's left of Chestnut Avenue. Children came from Clydebank and Cardonald for matchless auburn conkers. Until the dual carriageway smashed through, cleaving it in two, the avenue afforded the finest courting in the county; though I was always better at chestnuts.

By the shore, the Convent of the Good Shepherd is still there, where my mother, the nurse, wiped the floor with stoic humour for want of other work.

The tide's low. Between those posts, timber drifted with the flow. Now the useless pickets lurk like a weird and watery war grave. At West Ferry where we used to swim, the ferry had long gone west. Dan, the wily winger, played his football at Parklea. He could see the Highlands beyond the corner flag. Reckoned rickets improved his dribbling.

Then Woodhall: here Uncle Kenneth, the army boxer, punched tickets. Here Port Glasgow begins in earnest. Here's where I get off.

My mother's mother, Granny Quigg, the belle of Bally-castle, lies in wait with the rest of Spencer's spooks in the green graveyard that climbs the hill outside the station. Port Glasgow's resurrection is a little overdue. I've seen corner shops like the Gate of India before in the South Bronx, in South Central LA, but hey, there's no link between poverty and crime said a Government spokesman between mouthfuls of beefburger.

Mum's brother Uncle Frank lives in Woodhall Terrace. Aunt Anne's on the Glasgow Road, their close is clean, their renovated tenements pink with pride. The other surviving Quigg, the aforesaid Kenneth, didn't follow his siblings down the hill, he's still in Bardrainey in a well-kept modern row in that part of town developed after the Second World War. No hellos today, just private moochings. I'd climb to the house I was born in if it still stood; a dreich, damp, primrose-distempered council block, demolished these 20-odd years. Whoever had the blueprint, also had the rose-tinted specs: the port's as planned as an act of God. A vengeful god.

One of my kinsmen (through marriage merely), a bailie in the Fifties, was dubbed by a Scottish tabloid 'the man who walks alone' (in off-white sandshoes as it happens). He had a housing policy all his own – if you're Irish, come into the parlour. Relatives were jumping the queue like pole-vaulters. He was astonished when someone noticed. Did he get my dad that house in Broadfield? Uncle John, Robert, Sarah, all within soup-sniffing distance.

Robert was slow and a teaboy in his thirties. The men at Scott's Shipyard kept him around, a mascot, a charity case with brown, hurt eyes who died lobotomised and mournful. I have his as my middle name. Sarah wasn't all there. John was all there and everywhere wired and wiry, hedgehog-haired, 'a rare tear'. I used to sit on Robert's heavy shoulders and watch the traffic on the Firth. You could hear the yards for miles. Broadfield's smell was chip fat and rhododendrons.

AUCHENBOTHIE HOUSE WAS also 'up the hill'. To this old folk's home as assistant matron came Mary Hester Quigg aged twenty-eight, late of London and the Whitechapel Hospital. The entire family followed her over to the East End from Ballymena, when my grandfather dropped dead in

1952. Thus in 1957 came the Antrim Quiggs to Port Glasgow. And on a corporation bus Hester met Dan, a handsome wee man of nearly fifty. They argued ever after as to who spoke first. My money's on my father, all five foot of him. They were married within months, Mum in a most becoming pastel blue. If she had a past she never mentioned it to me. Nor was I the cause. Her first-born arrived prompt but proper on the first Sunday of the Greenock Fair, the July after that October.

My proud father was fifty by then. He'd tended to his mother's increasingly selfish whims after she took to the sherry and the *chaise longue*. Delusions of grandeur and grande-damery set in after my grandfather was crushed to death between two passing buses. He took a purple week to die. He'd been an inspector. His own transport company got started with a model T, moved on to charabancs until he sold out to a competitor. It was cars he liked, not commerce. To him, a steep town's cobbled braes were as heady and headlong as Klosters. His wife lived on, tragic and trying until the end. The funeral meats very nearly turned up as sausage rolls at the nuptials. Dan lost a mother and gained a wife. He was too old to mess about.

Walking into town from Woodhall, with the river at my right hand behind the rehabbed houses, I follow in my parents' footsteps, she tall and fat, he wee and slight, out for a saunter of a Sunday; improbably winching.

Dan was never your man for the melting word; was good at, but hated, writing. Yet when he died, a year after my mother, Maureen, my sister, told my brother Stephen and I of letters he'd sent mum from down south when he was working away for a stint. They're so adorably, damnably *tender* I can't read them. Bundled and tied, addressed to 23 Cairn Terrace, they're safe in my sister's keeping.

Cairn Terrace. The flats all flattened. The quarry quiet. Granny's room and kitchen was salty yellow butter, and a box bed for Aunt Anne, a toilet on the landing, ingenious bathing strategies; a wash house in the back court. We played *Rawhide, Cheyenne* and *Bonanza* on the blazing sandstone bluffs.

The ropeworks look Sarajevan. Newark Castle across the road is in infinitely better nick, despite its antiquity. Five hundred years on at least it's a going concern, *heritage* not birthright. Nowadays a job down here is no-one's right. At the

Gourock Ropeworks in the boom times and before nylon, nobody got money for old rope. Dad's older sister Lena gave a plaiting machine the finger and was stumped as to quite how or why for the rest of her gap-palmed life. For strangers, shaking her hand was an unforgettable experience.

Port Glasgow's reason was its river. It didn't exist; and so had to be invented. For the merchants of Glasgow a shallow river meant shallow purses. Ergo The Port of Glasgow. Port Glasgow. The Port.

When they learned how to dredge the river (in 1773), Port Glasgow was in deep trouble. Tobacco boats sailed serenely by. The locals spat in the Clyde, built ships and made rope. Places that don't make anything don't make sense.

Jobs or no jobs, Port Glasgow's still a working-class place. You could fit its entire middle class into just one patio, without breaking out the folding chairs or a second bottle of sauvignon blanc. By comparison with Port Glasgow, Wishaw is chi chi. In the rain the Port's as grey as anywhere I've ever been when not wrapped in a wet blanket. On a wet winter afternoon it's like being under a tea strainer.

Wit and weather go together. So down here humour tends to come in two varieties: gallows or black, a chesty chuckle in the face of ill fortune. This may be a West of Scotland cliché, another of poverty's sly excusing truisms. But it is true, triumphantly, transcendentally. Not end-of-the-pier, bottom-of-the-barrel, did-you-hear-the-one-about-humour . . . but rough and ready wit improvised out of, about and to *sustain*, everyday life.

I'd love to walk again with Dad in his beloved burgh's newest neat wee park. Modest and immaculately maintained, the Coronation Park rolls down to the water's edge, across the busy Greenock Road opposite the town centre. Just me and a wee boy and his dad fishing. Newark was a fishing village until Glasgow offered those 1300 merks (about £72) to construct its harbour, 1668 that was. Before that James IV would sail over to the Castle from his fortress in Dumbarton. 'The blissingis of God be Herein', it says on the lintel of Newark Castle.

The park was laid out in the depths of the Depression between 1930 and 1935. Those were hard days for my father and the other skilled men on Clydeside; unemployment affected eleven out of twelve workers in Port Glasgow. The Makework Park is built on landfall over the old West Harbour, already obsolete by the Twenties. It took a war to get the river moving again. Dan was too old and in a reserved occupation. He made munitions.

The Port's three high-rise blocks, Rowan, Thistle and Heather, blossomed in 1970. They are as ugly as you would expect. Their only rival is the towering peppermint green gantry of the Scott Lithgow Yard. Half of the group's shipyards were in Greenock, half in Port Glasgow.

The Port abuts but isn't Greenock (or Grin-ock, as news-casters would have it). One becomes the other without obvious demarcation. To the chauvinistic denizens of either, the other is utterly distinct. John Galt, who favoured Greenock, dis-missed the neighbouring burgh as Port Punch town. Port Glasgow's writer is James Thompson. Tom Leonard's magni-ficent biography makes clear how ambivalent his relationship was to his birthplace. The Port is a place apart. Greenock has its esplanade, IBM and yacht club. A good conceit of itself. I belong to Port Glasgow; am a Portonian; a cut below.

As a schoolboy I was big and fat and didn't know whether to be proud or ashamed of requiring the inside leg measuring ministrations of the gents department of the co-operative ('always the Co not the Co-op', such solecisms matter). Beds and the like came from Dunbar's Stores. The Co-op is kaput, Dunbar's is still there. The nearness of the Firth, its smells and gulls, were amazing to me, are extraordinary and evocative still. To look down Princess Street, the main shopping thorough-fare, and see the river and the hills of Argyll and a replica of the Comet just yards away, is stirring and not just to romantics and sentimentalists like me. Henry Bell's invention is dry-docked for posterity behind chicken wire in the car park, its heyday brief, its significance seminal for a working river lacking enough work to go round. I am not nostalgic for other people's sweat. When I hear Rod Paterson's beautifully un-ironic version of *The Song of the Clyde* I don't cry for *then* I cry for *now*.

The view from Birkmyre Park is worth the climb. Like much else in this very small town, it owes its existence to a magnate's magnanimity, in this instance that of the owner of the now defunct Ropeworks. There's a kempt, kenspeckle, well-used bowling green and in the bleary blue yonder, a vista to dazzle any visitor's eye. Aunt Lena lived up here and always took the view for granted. Dan delivering cans of milk before school in the early Twenties, never did. And it is beautiful, not just on a gouache gusty, April afternoon, with a low smoky light on the Firth and the smudged blue hills in the distance beneath a pearl and pewter sky. The tenements are beautiful. The derelict Doric columns on Jean Street School, beautiful, Barrs Brae. The Devol Glen. High Carnegie. Clune Brae. The Bogle Stone. Wallace's Loup. Beautiful every one. In or out of a Stanley Spencer painting.

At the turn of the last century that man of vision, Patrick Geddes, saw the need to balance Work, Place and Folk. Six miles upriver, George Wyllie has been asking all the right questions for years. Nowhere is the Geddesian trinity more fractured, the human balance more in need of restoration. Fine folk. A great place. But work? If Scotland doesn't know what to do with Port Glasgow, how will it know what to do with itself? I hope there will be a Parliament. I hope there will be answers. Looking out to where the river becomes its Firth, all I have to offer are the high hopes of spring.

I COULD HAVE GONE ON TO Gourock, to the end of the line, completed my journey, visited Dad's wise and funny sister Agnes, reminisced. But I was in Gourock just a week ago helping to bury her sister. So I had a pie in Aulds, bought 'a Tilly' (the *Greenock Telegraph*, dad's daily dose of home). I didn't cry into my beer in the bar of the Star Hotel, or have a fish supper at Louis's, or stick my foot in the doors, asking redundant welders 'how they feel'. I didn't 'pit oan' the Port Glasgow accent that was educated out of me. I bumped into Aunt Lena's daughter Vera, a good omen.

When I was asked what I wanted to be when I grew up, I'd always reply with deadpan precocity, a historian or a *mythologist*. My father's lanes are full of unreliable memories. The present should neither trust nor patronise the past. It's time to return to Glasgow, to go back, to go home.

1

A Letter from my Father

'When we are no longer children we are already
dead.'

Brancusi

'What things the young will take for songs or grief.'

W. S. Graham

CLOCKWORK

Broken clocks and watches were my father's hobby,
Killing time, he'd say, no irony intended, –
So grandfathers loitered dumbstruck in our lobby,
Hands salaaming as if begging to be mended.

Testimonial tokens of lifetimes on the job
Added to his pile their grateful mollusc gape.
Stammering snuff-stain waistcoat fob –
Tick corrected by puff and scrape.

Eyeglass squinched, he'd read the auguries,
Pronounce and whistle, arrange his tiny tools,
Wind the watch until we'd hear it wheeze,
Teaching me to prod among the cogs and spools

Though my cack-handedness loomed larger through his glass
He didn't mind the knack not passing on
It's a stoic's pastime, letting time pass,
He knew with quartz and plastic his day had gone

Now Dad's hands are slow and he's lost his spring
His face is scuffed by the emery-paper years
But he can value a clock by its pendulum swing
Or a watch, by the tact, of the tick, that he hears

And on Sundays sometimes we still repair
To smile at every bang on mantel chime
So many hunched gloamings unwinding there
My father and I keeping perfect time.

MILK

Your custom often
when the house was still

to brew milky coffee
and reminisce.

Child care experts would have frowned
on my late hours,

the bitter adult drinks
and frothy confidences.

Yet your stories stopped my mewling
and continued as I grew

me tending the fire,
you talking of Ireland,

more real to your first born
than the younger ones who slept.

Those nightcaps, Mother,
were our hushed bond.

And though, for twenty years now,
I've drunk my coffee black,

I'm not weaned yet
of that rich, warm milk.

PRIMARY

Every word I've ever read or written
I owe to you Miss Hughes –
dream colleen and crabbit queen
of primary one

With your round white face
and russet perm you could have modeled
Ireland for *The Book of Kells*

and green –
     your eyes
          and swankiest
               sweaters

green

the lightest
     brightest
          tightest
               green

Those first terms were mostly religion
sums and reading but you
grew hyacinths in the dark
curdling in that cupboard also
school milk into cheese.
Our first solid achievement.
Your muslin miracle.

It was 1964; we bought 'Black Babies'
wept and wet ourselves
but were excused –
Pees and Queues for the 'lavatory'
never the toilet
A stickler for proper English
and Catholic self-improvement
praying we'd pass for higher class
you spruced up where we came from
helped us out:

'Port Glasgow' was articulated sternly
and in full
                'The Port, Daniel O'Rourke
is vulgar
                teeth and tongue now, Porrtt
Glass go.'

You pulled out all the glottal stops
corrected nearly everything we learned
at home

Miss Hughes, you had magnificent breasts
and I loved you

You turned all our cream to crowdie.

TRIP

1   It's 1965 and on the Coast students
are high on mescalin and the Byrds.
Also on a coast, we are low
on lemonade and the Jaffa Cakes
can't last. En famille at Saltcoats,
five paddle and pinken on the *Our
Lady of Lourdes Parochial Trip
and Draw*. Almost exactly six, I've
a wee brother two years younger,
and beneath a bonnet, a new
sister, nine milky months old. My
mother and father speak in low voices
nearly touching. Out of the breeze
on a PVC tablecloth, we are
a knuckle.

2   Suddenly with a sob, Mum notices
her engagement ring is shy of a diamond –
one shiny grain among millions
on the sun spangled strand.
Burrowing like Bedouin

at a long dried up well,
we know it is hopeless. The crying
makes my sun burn sting and though Dad loves
a sing song, on the bus home
our family is quiet.
Then my sister wins the raffle . . .

3   Experiments show that acid dropped
in the 60s still ricochets around the blood,
latent, fickle, non biodegradable,
a chemical trip wire for the brain –
LSD flashbacks, causing old heads
momentarily to freak, for instance
on the freeway, a falcon pecking
at your eyes, or on Wall St
a broker still picking up the tab
for an open air concert he was
too out of it to hear.

4   I passed on drugs
yet repeatedly a trip comes back, bright and broken.
There's a family in it, hard to sunder
as the Ailsa Craig. It blows my mind
at the weirdest moments; has the splintered
clarity of sunlight prismed
in a beachcombed stone.

THE BEACH AT MAGILLIGAN

That buttermilk beach, the longest in Ireland
my mother trod in her Northern girlhood.

Now wire and watchtower skulk where she stood
guard over sandcastles: Magilligan Strand

where, behind a steel stockade, searchlights
comb the cells of Nissen hut anchorites.

THE DONEGAL DYNAMITERS

Sure I'll have a jar with you says Packie
For didn't I damn near build yon Hydro Dam
At Cruachan on me own – a powerful dram
Ye get in Scotland. Mind it's fierce tricky
Work dynamiting mountains, though I was
On the shovelling side meself – rare town
Glasgow, ye'll know the Gorbals; I lodged in Crown
Street with a Jewish widow's in laws –
Sounds Irish I know but there you are.
Did ye ever hear o Paddy Crerand?
Well he's a Donegal fella and
So was Patrick Magill, wrote a quare
Wheen about the Navvies so he did. Gave us pride.
A glow? That's just searchlights in the air –
No shortage of dynamiters over there,
Though these days, mostly on the shovelling side . . .

IN BALLYVAUGHAN (for Garry O'Briain)

Admiring the grain
And its sculpted curves

I ask about the table
'Oh I made that', you say

Planing across my gush
The way you'd trim a fiddle.

'Now who's for a bit of this'.
You field a goat's cheese lightly

In your big musician's hand
Our knives raised keen as hurleys.

VINCENT (for Manus McGuire)

Tonight Vincent the moon's a *bodhran*
Silent as yours is when the air needs calm
Then your bones are tactful

The Atlantic drumming into Galway Bay
In double jig time, beat light and steady
As yours is with the *Flowing Tide*

Head cocked quietly to Len Graham's song
Chocolate bar and can of *Lilt*
Atoll in a sea of stout

With a drum whose skin is thin as yours is
Whip round gift from the session men
And regulars of LINANE'S QUAYSIDE BAR

Did you learn those rhythms when your mother
Nearly drowned a few days before your birth
The beat of water about to burst the womb

Your slowness at all but drumming

ROBBIE

We shouldered you out into a cold blue morning,
the pig iron kind all keepers hate

when limbs get skinned and balls bound high.
There was a cross wind blowing from the Firth –

a day for inswingers; though corners
never troubled you who'd have got both hands

on the moon, given a two yard run at it.
No, your weakness was the fierce first timer

9

cleverly kept down, the only way we ever
got you out, playing 'Three and In',

on your well-kept Gourock lawn,
replaying the war years

when you were Cappielow's number one,
saving penalties like ration coupons.

To the *Telegraph* then, Robbie,
you were Morton's Miracle Man Between The Sticks,

invincible in polo neck and bunnet –
old goalie a league of ailments

couldn't beat, till a cunning cancer
aimed one low.

ALL LEAVE CANCELLED (for PC Stephen O'Rourke)

In the temporary mortuary
at the ice rink, you spent Christmas Day
body bagging those the pathologist's knife
had gourded. You'd asked us round and Life

Goes On . . . I carved the turkey in your absence
shirking comparisons. Dorothy was tense
the children muted – the crackers they pulled
imploding like a Boeing's pressurised hull

in the dead air space over Lockerbie.
While we scoured the floor for the debris
of a shattered toy, your colleagues searched
the Galloway Hills for fragments. Perched

on the edge of your empty seat we passed the day
resisting the emblems of Tragedy –
in cinnamon-scented candles and kitchen smells;
the reek of putrefaction – parallels.

10

JOHN SCOTUS ERUGENIA

Rain and gale
A sky that greys
To the Atlantic's
Doubtful blue
While in your cell
Of dour Liscannor stone
A fragrant candle licks
The manuscript's illumination
Italicised Latin
Dark as dolmens.
You skirt the homespun round
You, cowled against the cold
Gloss a speculation
Of Dionysius the Aeropagite.
Your stroke is sure.
Eyes are clear
With dreaming of the *Perigrinatio*
That begins tomorrow.
Will there be ale at Laon,
A bawdy jibe,
Graffiti at the Gospel's edge,
Or any Bard to harp a song
Or pipe;
'*All things that are*
And all things that are not' –

You still your quill
Lost in Plato fearful of pride
And heresy
Your *peryphrygeon* is planned
The first of its five
Provocative parts
Already written.
You are not yet twenty.
The bell for Compline sounds.

The Abbot's corrach waits.

SHAKY FOOTAGE (for Tina Wakerell)

At a dusty crossroads in the Twenties,
Step dancers slip through a neighbourly jig
In thick soled boots and outsize caps; Glenties
Maybe – the library shot list's vague,

Too soft for Donegal, Kerry say
Or slow West Cork. Eyes shyly on the ground,
Melodeon cradled like a day
Old lamb, head cocked to the long wiped sound

Of a fiddle, quick in brown slow motion,
A farm hand's fixed in shaky footage.
In the next shot, freeze framed against the Ocean,
A couple waltz by their cottage,

Gazing west past sud and skellig, to dance
Shoogly reels in green draped Brooklyn bars.
Cut to modern music their ghosts enhance
Our Gaelic rock show, become its stars.

BALLINTOY

Frank Quigg rests at Ballintoy
in loamy Protestant soil,
the North is truest here, loyal
to the lie of this land –
its ancient truculence of spume.
And Kintyre marks the spot I find my kin in:
you can see Scotland more clearly than ever it sees itself.
Beyond windy cottages blanched as linen,
in the Church of Ireland cemetery
my grandfather's memory I exhume,
seven years buried before I was born,
dowdy in mourning left on this coastal shelf
Scotland was torn
from.

12

'*Could I carry your wee parcel Miss Delargey?*'
that was how it started:
love got up in ribbons that never quite came undone,
though soon it was Annie who carted
the whiskey's burden
'*mixed fortunes in a mixed marriage –*
can you be surprised?' the Lambeg gossips said.
But there was passion and kindness, mostly Annie stayed.
Certainly my mother's father liked a glass;
but he left her always to early Mass.
And many's the hard word
and harder fist, Frank Quigg got
when drink ventriloquised an answer
to some Ballymena bigot,
until his second war took him away;
and sailing convoys out of Scapa,
he calmed, came to love the sea.

'*When I go Annie, lay me down here*',
he'd joshed one Sunday up the coast.
And so at Ballintoy he lies,
taken at his word, taken from Ballycastle
to this green place where most,
(in sober willing too), he'd wished his stone to stand,
on this adamantine, snaggle shored Antrim land.
And I see it first of a risen Easter Day
by a sun warm and low as the last orange nightcap
in a bottle of Bushmills:
looking to the land his women went to,
oh how the heart fills
with that older Scottish blood
that corrached Colmcille's sea
to Dalriada.
The Ulster blood that pulses proud in me
pounds pape and planter both
At Ballintoy Frank Quigg lies:
green and blue, the kyle's cold truth.

WHAT CELTS DO

The Ne'erday bottle of the Famous Grouse
Would last a year in my father's house
When he went for a pint
He always left it at one
He'd raise a worried glass to his thirsty son.

It's what Celts do
Fighting and drinking
It stops you
writing and thinking
It's true
I'm sinking
To the bottom of an empty glass.

I get flirty after one or two
I get shirty when I've had a few
I make phone calls I'll regret
Solemn promises I'll forget

It's what Celts do
Fighting and drinking
It stops you
writing and thinking
It's true
I'm sinking
To the bottom of an empty glass.

I like bath-tub gin and fine French wine
There's no bar bill I won't sign
I'm not embarrassed at drinking alone
Be it sawdust saloon or a lounge with tone

It's what Celts do
Fighting and drinking
It stops you
writing and thinking
It's true
I'm sinking
To the bottom of an empty glass.

I've widdled piddled, as all drunks will drool
Mumbled and stumbled with a tumbler full
I've burned my gut and I've boiled my brain
But if you insist, I'll have the same again.

It's what Celts do
Fighting and drinking
It stops you
writing and thinking
It's true
I'm sinking
To the bottom of an empty glass

CEOL BEAG (for Bill Currie)

He spanks it into life the squalling reel
that squeaks and twitters as we stamp shy feet.

Whisky leaps in tumblers and hearts in breasts,
the chanter tips its modal winks;

Glenorchy spraying grace notes
like a salmon trailing Spey . . .

vaulting through the twilight's spangle
out of blackness into blue,

a Scottish summer blue
pale and temporary. Beneath, a dark pool waits.

WA HEIDS

Frae thi French o Philippe Soupault

tae Tristan Tzara

Thi hail toun hiz cam intil ma chaummer
thi birks hae mizzled
an forenicht claps tae ma fingirs
Thi hooses ur turnin intil Clydebuilt Cunarders
thi soun o thi sea hiz jist raucht me here, up by
In twa daws we'll win till thi Congo
Ah've passed thi equator an thi Tropic o Capricorn
Ah ken there ur undeemous braes
Sanct Mungo derns thi Gaurisankar an thi Merrie Dancers
nicht fa's drap bi drap
Ah wyte fur thi oors

Gie me yon ginger an a last cigarette
Ah'm gaun back tae Glesca

TWENTY OR SO

On blue nights in Glasgow
We'd lie on the floor
And smile as John Martyn
slipped under the door

Bird'd be blowin
Lennie'd be Cohen
And we'd all be goin'
On twenty or so.

Our hair it was longer
The wine was much stronger
And nobody studied T.V.
We wore combat jackets
Wrote songs on fag packets
James Taylor would put on L.P.

16

Bird'd be blowin
Lennie'd be Cohen
And we'd all be goin'
On twenty or so.

Man it was great
Back in 78
Before we'd the key to the door
Thatcher's ambition
Had not begun pishin
On all that we dreamed and hoped for.

Bird'd be blowin
Lennie'd be Cohen
And we'd all be goin'
On twenty or so.

We'd stroll the West Quad
like we owned it by God
Look down on the city below
We were always in love
Safe up above
There was nothing
That we didn't know.

Bird'd be blowin
Lennie'd be Cohen
And we'd all be goin'
On twenty or so.

Ach to be young
With the tang on your tongue
Of Leonard and Morgan and Gray
Beer in your belly
Football on the telly
And no more exams until May.

Bird'd be blowin
Lennie'd be Cohen
And we'd all be goin'
On twenty or so.

ANGUS IN HIS 80s

In this peaty, puddled land
his spade's excalibur;
at eighty-six, still claiming crop
from gale and sucking bog.
The Atlantic's a skiff away –
blue black as plums:
with hair like spume
and in gansey and denims,
he's a fierce tide going out.

CRYSTAL

I had forgotten how tiny the glasses were;
a house of sticky Christmas drinks.
Glugging whisky into mugs I see you grue
at Tio Pepe presented in error
so many long first foots ago
before we learned of drams or death –
cups too bitter for liqueur glasses:
that crystal is all I'll take
from this house we've come to close.

WILDLIFE ON ONE

At the end of his life
my dad the square-eyed townie
watched wildlife programmes mostly:
a jackal gnaws on a living gnu's
hindquarters, a crocodile clamps
its implausible jaws around a dazed gazelle
at a waterhole while the
dripping herd bolts off.
Dad knew what orchids eat
The way a snowgoose flies
How gibbons get in spring
Golden eagles were as familiar

18

to him as whaups or hoodies, angelfish
blazed across his Clyde
caribou mooched on
the moonlit moors of Renfrewshire
hiding or hungry in the snow.
Dad loved the telefoto zoom,
fast film stop frame,
Grizzly close ups in sly slo mo
Never got used to David Attenborough though.

PRAISE BE

About your 'interior life'
I never heard a cheep –
what's certain is that
those Victorian spooks,
your parents never made
a man of you
with their huffs and hurricanoes
They thought *cuddled* meant coddled.
Love's like iron to the
growing boy
a baffling necessary abstraction.
On the shopfloor keeping
in the 'good books'
of 'big shots', and 'heid bummers'
was a point of pride with you.
That you *were* so good
at your job made
Grimm Tales at teatime,
of plaudits from the brass
seem so much paternalistic guff.
No inconsistency between
your political beliefs
and this fawning fondness for a toff's soft soap
ever crossed your bright but narrow mind.
You loathed kow-towers, tongue and bum
men on the make. In the course of that
gruff Port Glasgow rearing, when

19

you weren't being raised
between 1910 and the Depression
only God was praised.

A LETTER FROM MY FATHER

It's extant only on official forms –
the wee coiled writing of my father.

His copperplate chalked on corporation
slate was lyric, legible, neat.

On tax returns its furls and curlicues
were daintier far than *Carolingian Miniscule*.

Yet he hated writing and many's the chit
or docket I penned for him

in the naïve scrawl that prints these lines.
Through all my journeyings, small triumphs

and reverses
I never had a note from him; whatever

needed telling, he was more inclined to say.
Slicing through the post these mornings

how I crave a letter from my father,
paternal greetings in a flawless script.

2

The Waistband

'I just want to tell y'all not to worry – them people in New York and Hollywood are not going to change me none.'

Elvis Presley, 1956

'Life's like Sanskrit read to a pony.'

Lou Reed, *What's Good*

DEAR ANDREW McGREGOR

I've become my mum –
wireless on all morning
not Wogan or Clyde
for me but Radio Three
and you Andrew McGregor,
whose name I growl
with its gritty, rolling, Rob Roy
'Rs' a great big gruff
hairy and heroic name
trailing gravel and burrs –
though you yourself have mild
Tony Blair style vowels and Home
Counties headnotes: a high
nuzzling whinny that seems
to say 'Nanny, can I
have a sugar lump?'
I'd give you a sugar lump:
I'd give you two! Andrew
are you medium height,
slight, thinning in your thirties,
I know you cycle in;
you told me. Bet it's not
a mountain bike. Bet you!
I used to get up with you
at seven; now we both start
at the crack of six.
Dear Andrew, this is not
some foolish fad of mine.
My dial's spinning!
My aerial's up!
If I've guessed right about
you, send me a sign:
make your third piece on
Thursday, the misterioso
movement from Furtwangler's
pre-war recording of
Bruckner, symphony number nine.

AMENITIES (for Pauline Law and Allan Campbell)

Approximately 9.01, a Wednesday

First week in May
sun on the sandstone
a little extra butter
on one's eggs (figure-
atively speaking – no
cholesterol for me) –
tan shorts, teal tee-shirt, sandals
out for a paper
and some air

                      no London

news

          this a.m.
             times

is tight, if beautiful
I'm even whistling, so
so

      sincere words at Kelvin
bridge

      with eyes down young T.V. guy'd
sooner slope on by
than swap amenities with one
so flagrantly

             former

Cooler he'd rather

           warmer

I get, point even of
pinching his cheek
Give my love to any who remember
A lazy left on Otago
Coffee steeping

         this poem

starting
The blue sky

        The by-gones

FRIDAY LECTURE

1.
On every page Norman MacCaig
had a good conceit,

Of himself
above all —

Call it a modest vanity,
a smiling scowl —

A whole parade of paradoxes
kicking up their heels.

The amiable drams with cronies
notwithstanding, if he found you foolish he'd

enfilade you with a word —
Oh his objections were conscientious no doubt —

He and the big abstractions wouldn't serve,
he was his own country;

himself the only call he ever answered.
Poems ran out of puff after a single fag.

Academics knew hee haw. He saw
the world from contrary angles.

MacCaig could stravaig
the world with a glance

Seeing was *being*

2.
In the Glasgow Film Theatre
I feed the five hundred at
The Art School's Friday lecture
I'm not the main feature, MacCaig is

25

Part projectionist, part ice-cream vendor
I read him (we *need* him and his dry
droll drawl) and talk about the great man
and his great works, the life, the times,
the two spurned baffling early books, another, debut
at forty-five; his masterpiece *Surroundings*
at fifty-six. He allowed
the influence of only two: John Donne
and Wallace Stevens. I read a poem
by each – proof or reproof? To
call in an unpaid debt I throw in
A Martian Sends a Postcard Home
an I.O.U. Craig Raine forgot to sign.
For an hour I exhume, expatiate, explain
Apolitical, classless, classical, urbane
Then again, a Gael in 3/4; of his
blood and all his brain:
Scalpay and Lochinver, Bruntsfield and the
Links, a diligent life spent in primary schools
primarily of poems, malt and
verses in the evenings: a book
every other year. Even detractors admit
the wit was Marvellous, the
optimism infectious, a communicable disease.
He could be as sentimental as a
music box but the poems he made
for his dead best friend were tears, wreath
eulogy and wake.
For their sake
alone, I'd love his *Collected Poems*.

OH I HAVE SUNG WANTONNESS
(for Madeleine MacLaverty)

In Novo Sibersk in spite of
thirteen sorts of vodka
In Pilsen between Budvaars
before the velvet revolution
On the train from Kassel
to Weimar just before the
border
After drawing with the Auld
Enemy at round about
Kilmarnock
In Regent's Park
At a US Embassy barbecue
In any Irish county
bar Armagh
In Estonia, Finland, Norway
always in the midnight sun
On the Studs Terkel show
in Chicago
For Sverige Radio, one Burns Night
In a Frank Lloyd Wright
bungalow in Michigan
a semitone too high
At the Scotch Malt Whisky
Society as part of my toast to the 'Lassies'
a semitone too low
In a kayak on lac du verre
in Quebec
In the Rainbow Room (sotto voce)
On the quay in Greenock
Burns would have sailed from
On top of Ben MacDui
At the bottom of the Grand Canyon
At the drop of a hat
Acht who needs a hat!
In my very own flat
whenever the occasion demanded
Sometimes when it *didn't*

At weddings
Funerals
A christening (once)
At my own 21st
Along with Jean Redpath
Along with Rod Paterson
At the feet of Hamish Henderson
In to myself
Hundreds of times for Burns
Once or twice for me.

SCOTTISH COLOURISM

These are the good days
poems
        piling
                up
                        nicely
living simply
            simply
        living
                    in all this sun
            while May
rattles its tin at June
like a Swedish flag
                    day
but 'Scotch' tomatoes
                    to
                        slice
                            with
                                    salt
on rough rye toast
(a healthy re-
spect these days for heart disease, etc)
leaving the cork
in the wine bottle a while
apricots and tea and
books of an afternoon
mornings of work

you wish would never end
as if a favourite
                Freeling Simenon or Chandler
Odd intervals on the blond guitar
convivial and exacting as
Li Po's lute. Solitude and
old friends
phone calls few, but festive
finally,
finely,
the essential balance
If you will
'The Way'
what I had in mind anyhow when
I told the aye sure sceptics
that I meant it
about the change
This incomparable lazy,
                May –

                    zy

month's and evening
while I walked
between the sun smoored
hours of 6 and 8
my loggings were
            Wych Elm
            Sycamore
            White Alder
                and
            The Common
            Lime

Blinded by blossoms in the
Oriental dell at the Kelvin's
edge, a young woman and her boyfriend
rehearse a Driving Test viva.
From the bridge on Kirklee Road
While the gloaming coyly folded itself
like a fan
I gawped up at the window

in which repatriated from the
Riviera, J. D. Fergusson
laid it on thick
for his Japaneasy women.

IT'S SO BEAUTIFUL TONIGHT YOU WISH

you could stroll by the Thames near Richmond
with Richard Price and his
brammer of a wild wee daughter Katy

or

loll by the lake (sans Calvin)
with Peter McCarey, in Geneva

eat any fruit but 'strawberries'
on Eddie Morgan's balcony
right here in the splendiferous
West End of Glesca

loup aroon the Marais wi big Davie Kinloch
spikin the bienliest o Marie Stuart Froag
an slorpin claret

introduce the Alans, Sharp and Riach,
the pair attempting tae rescue Scotland
with long lines from New Zealand

tour Fife with Professor Robert Crawford
and a walking stick he could use
as a pointer
'*Just cataloguing the culture, Constable* . . .'

promenade along the esplanade
slugging lemonade (ginger!) from the bottle,
in Greenock with a specially
flown-in Raymond Friel

mosey round Ferguslie with Graham Fulton
and a plausible explanation. Our talk
(a rib tickling double header) is entitled
Papes and Prods: Two
Paisley schools — six helpfully
maimed writers

play scratch football on the Meadows
with Ron Butlin and two teams of bards
who just happened to be passing

                              or

Just sit here till sunset listening to Lohengrin
defying things to get any better
Exhorting them to try.

FOR JAMES SCHUYLER

This morning in the New York Times
I read that you had died

over in St Vincent's a block
from where I drank my coffee

on West 10th Street and 7th
Avenue, the same place

they took Dylan Thomas, his liver
bursting with whiskey though

you'd been dry for years, just had
a stroke was all and died, quietly,

prosaically like your poems. You'd
a life and got it down; paintings, music,

men you'd loved. It had John Ashberry
and Frank O'Hara in it and despite it all,

31

New York. Browsing in the Saint Mark's Bookstore
the other day, not knowing you were sick,

I bought the book they gave you the Pulitzer for.
Ten years ago, so full of death and shriving.

I'll write the date in it and in memoriam.
It's good. I'll mind you by it.

New York, April 13 1991

(ANOTHER) LITTLE ELEGY

I
From the start
I liked the sound of you
liked your 'R s'
The best of west of Irish names
Frank O Hara
A quarter pirouetting
On the counter
Of a varnished bar O'Hara
ra ra ra ra ra ra ra ra –
Martini barman
Soon's ya like.

II
Charm harbours harm
it's word play, it's sword play

when the n'th martini's smarting
in the raw, ruined, brain
Joan Fontaine
      versus
         Olivia De Havilland
Bette Davis and Joan Crawford mano a mano
over a man oh
      that was Frank
           rank
when he drank

pissing off pals kissing off gals
who inspired, no sired,
his tenderest musings

Up most nights until the whites of daybreak's
eyes were muzzy in his sights
Then, whether in love or no,
a blow
      job for
            the straightest
                black
guy still standing

III

You so loved Russia − its vastness and its vodka
Steps could have been Steppes
the troika carrying Zhivago into the freezing Urals
where he'd chitter out his epitaph, the poems;
alone with a lantern and the wolves

Pasternak persisted as you did

You weren't like Mayakovsky

stumbling into the unreliable light,
decreed obsolete by your terrible talent.
You knew Yevtushenko for a phoney and a flunky
a sanctioned drone. In your vivace verses
Scriabin and Glazunov improvise brilliant moon lit
duets on an ice piano, until on Second Avenue,
they're joined by Prokoffiev and Tchaikovsky
in a mad and ardent passacaglia for eight hands.
Rachmaninoff needs another thousand poems
before you go off your rocker. Kruschev is coming
but on the wrong day. I hope in Heaven
you will get to know Mandelstam

I suppose he shines there; like stars, like snow

IV

I slowed down on West 10th at University
Place muttered *timber* Yup the
Cedar got the chop or was transplanted
three doors down, *Cedar* now in
name and nothing else a sort of
Bavarian Beer Keller cum Cowboy
bar singlesy, low lit –
Franz Kline wouldn't be seen
dead there (no matter how
thirsty he was)
Motherwell wouldn't bother hell
could freeze over before even
Pollock'd breeze over for a beer.
In the photographs it's all laughs and liquor round
rough plain tables or at
the old style polished counter
where you'd catch De Kooning's Dutch
courageous eye in the mirror behind the bar,
sloshing ice cubes in a double bourbon,
eager to announce Manhattan's newest marvels to
the men and women who were making up its myth.

V

The Atlantic is shilly shallying on the shore
An early gull or two, the party goers
Giggling or flirting or staring silently at the sound
The last of the moonlight
and midsummer's startling stoic stars
Summer 2/3rds gone
Another drunken dawn on *Fire Island*
Later, a hangover bourbon in your
juice: now you're hanging on
to the night and all its bright possibilities
Yet you are no longer young
Forty's the finish of so many lovely things
Will you choose boys and booze
over poems and a culpable prime
Halfway home the beach taxi's broken down
The tide's about to turn

Fire Island burning on
For your walk I fancy you chose the self same
glossy stretch of beach you etched that elegy on
in memoriam James Dean
A Porsche A Spyder now that's a car crash
An auto wreck featuring a beach buggy
is just too grotesquely frivolous, too kitsch, *too camp*
like Herbie the love bug in a hit and run
No! a comical jumped up pop art jeep.
Frank, sober you'd have seen that cheap
irony coming, seen it a mile off.

IN THI WARLD'S HERT

Frae thi French o Blaise Cendrars

Fun fragmint

This Glesga lift, mair claen nor winter sky, skyrie, bricht, wi
    cauld —
Ahve nivvir seed nicht sae starnie, mair bouzie, nor this spring
Wi boulevard birks lik scarrows o heiven,
Wappin wracks in garths gurged up wi elephant's lugs,
Wechtie conkers, blades o plane trees —

Whitelie watter lily-oak oan thi Clyde, mune shewn wi
    watter's threid,
Mulkie Wey in thi sky dreeps doon oan Glesca, smoorichs
Thi toun, doitit, tapsel teerie, mou sookin Kentigern's kirk.
Daddie Bear an Bairnie Bear scrunge aroon sanct Enoch's,
    gurlin.
Ma champit aff haun skinkles in thi skies — in Orion.

In this sail snell licht, chitterin, mair nor orra,
Glasca's lik thi jeelit parrymauk o a plant
That kythes againe in its shinners. A downie simulacrum.
Straught anglit, ivvir youthie, thi biggins an loans ur ae
Stane an steel, bingit up, ane unco desart.
Babylon, Thebes, nae mair deid thi nicht, nor thi
    deid city o Glesca

Blae, green, inkit, tarry-macadamit, its banes bleacht in star licht.
Soun: neither hishie nor wishie, nae fouter o fitfa at a. Thi
    lourdie sauch o war.
Ma ee swarves frae privvy tae purpie ee o causey leerie:
Thi wan glaik wey gat Ah maun trauchle ma fyke intil.
An thon's thi wey Ah stravaig Glesca ilka nicht,
Frae Kelvinbrig tae thi Calton, corsin thi Andes
Ablow thi glister o brent new starn, gretter, mair kittie:
Soudren Rood mair bi ordinar wi ilka step ye tak towards it
    Clims oot o thi auld warld
Aboon thi new continent.

Ahm thi cheil whas run oot o byganes. Ae ma scrunt
    mishampers me noo.
Ah've feued a chaumer in a howff, tae bide alane wi masel,
A sprang-new rubbage creel tae eik up wi manuscrips.
Nae buiks, nae picters, nae whigmaleeries tae grattifie me.

Dask stowed wi newsprint,
Ah scodge in this empie dunny, ahin a blin windae,
Barfit, oan rid Kirkcaldy flarin, Ah pley keepie uppie wi a
    baloon,
    a bairn's bugle.
Ah chaave oan THI FEENISH UP O THI WARLD

REVIEWING (for Peter Nardini)

> 'A good critic is one who likes as much as possible as
> persuasively as possible.'
>
> Randall Jarrell

Back in the 80s
when I was a would be Wolfe
two fingering it
on the *Herald's* Arts Desk
doing crits, laying
down the law acht
I had a certain something
    no doubt

turning phrases on a threepenny bit
Olympian in my twerpish 20s

All those stabs at stardom
each callow, crack
the injudicious mots justes

I take it all back

MESSAGES

After rehearsals all day I leave Glasgow's CCA
And walk west on Sauchiehall (St). It's cool for May
(*way* cool) but bright; the light is lavish
On the thirsty fountain at Charing X, where yellow spurts
And sparkles, nearly flooding the West End Park
(Aka Kelvingrove). Although there's a vivid hour til dark
Ages actually, I need the street beneath my feet
the nooks and knolls of record shops with a
Funky retro beat and bent: the Saturday's I spent, with
Ear muff headphones on listening to new Bruce Cockburn
Imports, or early country rock in the *23rd Precinct*
The wizard was wrong: you *can* go back sometimes, for a while
And all for the price of a classic re-issue bargain bin C.D.
Like Rickenbacker Roger (nee Jim) McGuinn's first solo LP
    which
I acquired in '73. Old Rog is in town next week but I won't be.
He never should have wiped Gram Parson's vocals off
Tambourine Man. These days I don't shop much, have more than
I need for more than halfway through this flâneur's life of mine.
On a stored up whim I'll take music home with me and wine
A long thin pointy loaf of Edinburgh baked French bread, Yves
    Klein
Coloured Irises, Berryman's *Dream Songs* or perhaps Gide's
journals instead, or any *Black Sparrow* book
Smith's have had the wit to stock. Some shops have cash back
Facilities because Capitalism wants our love not just our loot.
Whereas once it was only THURSDAYS, now any old night
    is Late

37

Opening. Idle but missing nothing, at almost thirty-eight,
I stroll on.

Hopeful and happy at the thought
of what's been bought
I'll lug my parcels home –
These *messages*;

And write.

BUTTONING IT

If life was insouciance
In a Breton sweater
I'd be living
running rings round it
except I can't seem to get it
over my Mt Rushmore
sized head.
                   Just as well
I kept my cardigan.

THE WAISTBAND

If you don't stop soon
you'll end up gross and penitent
like some wire jawed
sack of slurry
with a stapled gut
spilling it on the tea-time
talk shows how
'people of size' are gonna sue
the car manufacturers
the airlines,
the funeral parlours
for cutting it fine –
the right to be roomy
and twenty odd stone

in a Corvette
on a Boeing
in a glass topped magenta catafalque

wearing quaking polyester
is
the
right
to be
       a fat bastard
       a grazer on grease
       a waddling gullet
frankly a glutton
if one may resort to
    theology
the game's up Porky
your mirror is telling you
the scales are telling you
between mouthfuls of cheeseburger
Elvis in nappies is telling you

EVERTHING IS TELLING YOU

now go ask the fridge

THE LOVE SONG OF DANIEL O'BESE

First my gone gaunt love made my weight
an ultimatum; and then a *casus belli*.

SLAINTE BRENDAN (for Frank Quigg)

Aff kilter
        wan evening
                        wi drink
plooterin roon the kitchen
eftir
        (huvin hud)
eftir
        (lookin fur)
                                WINE!

Ah asked the inamorata
O the moment which
O the Eye-rish writers
Oan ma Eye-rish writer's
Calendar ah maist resembled
In ma a' too evident
Eye-rish writerness
                        secretly
hopin fur Flann O'Brien
wi ee's eyebrows an Trilby,
Whit ah goat but
                        wuz Behan
which sobered me
                        up.

FOR IAN CHARLESON

        'Horatio, I am dead;
        Thou liv'st; report me and my cause aright
        To the unsatisfied.'

I had to ask at the interval if
It was really you your film star looks worried
To the bone, EATING THE AIR PROMISE CRAMMED . . .
Wan and wasted, your pale eyes puffed
With grief – a sinus operation,
The programme seller said, she thought your Prince
Definitive, warned me that I'd weep . . .

40

THE VERY AGE AND BODY OF THE TIME . . .
Youthful still at forty, lapping doubt like
Liddell.
Staccato. Minims crushed to crotchets in your lyric
Urgency; sublimities spat out like so much gristle
I DO NOT SET MY LIFE AT A PIN'S FEE . . .
Nor could our bravos set such playing's worth . . .
The grave you hurried to was real – yours in truth,
THE HEART ACHE AND THE THOUSAND NATURAL
SHOCKS THAT FLESH IS HEIR TO . . . A bare month later,
When I read that you were dead, your last words
To Horatio came back and that television Burns
Night, when you sang
A Red Red Rose; and I and half of Scotland cried.

KEROUAC

On another fire escape in the Village
A red plaid shirt is drying
While your latest angel
Types uptown for groceries
A letter in her purse
Postmarked Tangier

You rinse the road off
In her coldwater room
Sucking at a pint of Thunderbird
Dreaming of kif and California

Cheered touchdowns in the Columbia yard
The deserts you call collect from
Nickels dropped in truckstop booths
Long loinsy letters from cantinas
In the adobe border towns
Begging her to join you
That this time it'll last

Tonight you'll tune her crystal set to Symphony Syd
Black Celt hair loam in her fingers
She'll search for love in eyes of Breton blue

As the office clock hits five
She dreams of finding you just once
Sober and happy to see her
After the bounce in from some cactus airstrip

Ardent still as when you wrote.

THE ROOMING HOUSES OF AMERICA

I'm the Stranger
the locals call Himself
holidaying wryly
off season in Donegal
sporting tweeds
reading detective novels
being found fascinating.

I'm the Poet
with hair en brosse
idling over pastries
in the Cafe Sperl
gossiping about the Opera
considering an intrigue
with a Frau in furs.

I'm the Drifter
in loose bruised jeans
riding blue rails
stealing guitar licks
from the widows of Jazzmen –
my only luggage
a pre war Remington

for the novels I tap out drunk
in the rooming houses of America.

INDEPENDENCE DAY

The last of Indiana, and it's Union Station
ten o'clock and Chicago free.
I've bumped 2,000 miles from New York City
in a kind of aluminum tomb
with martinis and the oiled counsel
of coronaries. How can such shirts bloom
so far north of Honolulu? The sun
from the observation car came down
like the last curfew in El Salvador on
Pennsylvania's miracle of unremarked ore,
then dinner with a Polish girl
from Connecticut on her way south
to be a nun. When I talked her into another
split of wine, I blushed
like Vlad the Impaler, turned out we both
liked Bessie Smith: '*Walking back to Chicago,*
Yessir that's what I'm gonna do . . .'
All the stewards were black and sassy
'specially Amlise my sleeping car attendant
who opened a stiff-topped bottle sweetly
with her teeth: 'It's the gold as does it . . .'
All night through the mauves and navies
of a midwest gridded like that dark Ad
Reinhardt in the Museum of Modern Art.
After a night's lame progress on my Frank O'Hara
piece, when it went up the sun ascended
like an orange fielded in a child's thirsty joy.
That was in Indian country, a little after five . . .
I tugged the blankets to me against the air
conditioned chill, warmed my hands on the embers
of a wagon train's dawn fire, thought of Sandburg,
Bellow and the wide words of their Lake,
then suddenly 10 am and a damp 103,
all the city downtown, laughing at Brits, so
the Tamil cabbie went the long way round.
Later my host drove me all over the city.
This room's on the twenty-third floor
with a full view of the Lake. I absorb that

and this silver cocktail, thinking of a novice,
wishing I had a vow.

Tomorrow I'll be thirty-one

July 4, 1990

ALGREN

I picture you profiled in Film Noir tones
shirt-sleeves rolled back, cigar smoke

coiling like an unpent spring
as you type at a card table

in some Clark St. cathouse
in '48 or '49

before Korea and McCarthy
made it hard for Reds to work.

The book you're writing,
The Man with the Golden Arm

will make a movie star of Sinatra
and not one royalty cent for you

last of the bare-knuckle poets,
more famous in the end

for being the first man
to make Simone de Beauvoir come

than for anything you wrote.
Travelling to Chicago

and later, here in the burg
you called a busted flush

I read, *The Neon Wilderness*
and *City on the Make*

serenades to the low lives
and losers of these streets.

As well, after your hobo
wanderings, the time you did

for stealing a typewriter,
that you remained constant to Chicago

her soda jerks and crap games
pastures new then

reduced to scuffed
green baize.

SECOND CITIES

It's 1902 and Glasgow is flourishing.
Only Chamberlain's Brum is her radical peer.
Newly Edwardian the braw baillies toddle
among the neat rhododendrons of their well
laid out parks. Clear from Loch Katrine
to the Delft sinks of Springburn, through municipal
lead, the soft water flows. And on tiled Gorbals
stairheads' new gas-mantles mutter while
electric light flickers in some single ends.
Dank dunnies and vennels demolished by bye-law
fester only in photos Thomas Annan exposed now that
cholera and typhus have been sluiced from the privies
by brisk MOHs of a socialist bent.
And in shipyard and foundry the healthy make money
for patrons to spend on donatable art.
Progress can be engineered; and St Rollox has the template
the future runs on tram-lines undiverging and true.
But they don't know what to make
of their Art Nouveau art school: so Mackintosh sulks

45

on a mauve straight-backed chair, while
acclaimed in Chicago, Wright fills Oak Park windows
with the same long-stemmed blooms in the same pastel shades.
Lake Michigan listens to Clydeside.
In the field of onions, great skyscrapers grow.
Intent on Utopia, they've made Glasgow their model.
So delegations ascend in their plainsduster coats
to survey our grey Eden from the top decks of trams
not minding the soot on the civic ideal.
And the Euphrates foams at Kelvinbridge. For a year
the *Tribune* billets a special correspondent
at London rates in the Central Hotel.
The George Square panjandrums pat their paunches
and whistle when Mayor Dunne wires the Provost
in fraternal good form, 'We are building in Chicago
the Glasgow of America'; then poaches Dalrymple
to make his trams run on time.

ALIBI

As I pause beneath the Wrigley Building
to bid the river a last good-night,
a pleasure boat called *Innisfree* putters
gaily towards the Lake, her tannoy
namechecking buildings I pan my neck to see.
Everyone else is at home with milk
and crackers, watching garbage on TV.
Me, I should be working on my alibi
in the city's low-life bars so that when
Mr. Ness calls round in his bullet-proof sedan,
there'll be a dozen witnesses to say Nuts to you Fed,
and swear it wasn't me.

BACK IN CHICAGO

'Gathered for cocktails in our studio tonight
are Elliot Ness, Al Capone, Ernest Hemingway
and General George Armstrong Custer.'
The latter fusses with his pony-tail
and a glass of pale, iced tea while special
agent Ness sips sarsparilla, coolly
declining the sanguinary Corvo Al's mama
used to like – (*Always bring your own,
that way they can't poison you, right*).
Papa drinks neat bourbon, not troubling with a glass
and insists on handing round a snapshot
of a half-ton marlin
he landed off Key West.
Custer claims he caught a bigger one
with a pike rod and a diaper pin . . .
Ernest ignores this, touching his empty bottle
to Capone's full glass. Gangster and writer drink
to shorter sentences. Ness does not join in.
Still wearing his homburg, the Untouchable
glowers at my stiffish gin and french.
All four pack pistols:
(Hemingway's is especially large!)
'Gentlemen', I begin, 'perhaps you could tell the viewers
how it feels to be back in Chicago'.

STUDS

To show she isn't clement always
Chicago sends a day of squalls.
But the clouds do not stay sombre.
Driving north on Lakeshore, the harbour's
permanent is blue-rinsed by the sun
as tenderly between oldies a phone-in DJ sells
the discounted contents of the nation's malls.

The cab pulls in to a tranquil street
of handsome brick, where burly still,
a little bowed, you shoo me in with quick, gruff
grace to a house homely in prosperous prairie style.
We talk in a petalled window drenched in primrose
light: in this oblong calm of Art Nouveau
your tales aren't tall, just true.

You tell me that Chicago is the City of Hands,
splaying your own broad pair,
cigar emphatic as a squat third thumb.
Polish hands, boning stockyard steers . . .
German hands, splashed by tubs of ore . . .
Irish hands, hefting a billystick's weight . . .
Black hands, artful on guitars . . .
But in the town you call
'Johannesburg on the Lake', there's dirtier work to do.
In the City of the Deal, the hands that shake to seal
are white, and fast bucks mortgage a slow decline.

But what's good is great and there's no-one prouder
of what was and will be in the city's myth.
I spend the morning listening to you
who listened to America: posterity's cocked rapt ear.

When at the door you say you'll sign
and send me your latest book, your spanner handshake
is your bond in bone.
                                        All the way downtown
I hear your kindly growl. So, the old days

48

were not always good and nostalgia's
history having a damned good cry but nightly
at your microphone you keep the 'ago' in Chicago.
It's the city's own true voice then
that drifts in quiet blue curls
like stogy smoke over the stockyards
as you play Big Bill Broonzy records,
from a real estate tower

MUSICK EFTIR A READIN

Frae thi French o Valery Larbaud

Eneugh wurds, eneugh sentences! O rael lif,
   Ertless an wioot metaphor be mine.
Coorie intil ma airms, dandle oan ma knee.
Come intil ma hert, come intil ma lines, ma lif.
Ah see ye afore me, wuppin, nae hinnered at a,
Like a loan in thi blessit Sooth, nairrae an warm,
Swarvin atween sic high hooses, whas taps
Dook intill thi ee'nin sky, wi
Saft-fleein flittermice skiffin bi them;
Causey lik a muckle, parfumit, vennel
O a Barrio del Mar whas neebor is thi sea richt eneugh,
An whaur in thi lown daurkness, in a wee meenit,
Thi serenos will chaunt thi oors lik psaulms . . .

But ma lif, yon's eyeways this causey oan thi nicht afore
Sanct Joseph's Day, whan thi whistlebinkies,
Geetars ablow their plaidies, stravaig an strum:
Verra peerie, oan thi laggan o sleep ye'll hear
thi soun o streengs an wuid, mair douce nor slaff itsel,
Sae chitterin, sae joyfu, sae sappie an sae slidderie,
That gin onlie Ah wiz tae tweetle
A thi Pepitas wad birl ceilidh lik in their scratchers:

Fegs naw!
Scronachs smatter ma sang! Ma ain sang!
(Ye urnae thi wan, America, yer loupin lins, yer wapple wuids

Whaur thi comin Spring tremmles, ye urnae thi wan,
Gret sauch o thi wunnersome lanely Andes,
Nupt, ye urnae thi wan wha fills this hert
Wi a consort ayont words, mixter maxeterin
Bowsterous delicht an sabs o pride . . .)
Acht! Gin Ah could ae gang whaur naebody bides, faur frae buiks,
An lat yon lyrical baist loupin in ma breist lauch an yammer!

LA POESIE/POETRY

La poesie, is
abstract as clams
in a cloudburst
or the width of wine
in a tight corner
                Poetry
Is sour skinned,
just so, so just,
ample as the cusp
we're beckoned by
               and love.

STRAVAIGIN

How's this for £4.95
bean and pasta broth
(so spicy, so sustaining)
in its big blue stripey bowl
followed
      discreetly
   (not snappily)
by Japanese ling
with chili and coriander
          and
(this is the bit you can't buy
comes extra like the wine)
the taste and testimony

of Richard Price:
sharp and musky
as the Catalan white

Gibson Street
Dec 5, 1994

MEASURES

I'm drinking too much
like my sherry sweet granny
like my mother's father in Ireland

like my namesake cousin
who died of it
like my favourite Uncle Frank
who didn't
           not alcoholic not
utterly dependent
just drinking too much
making
regrettable phone calls

saying things at parties
I'll blush to take back
getting flirty or shirty
just drinking too much
and the wagon's not the answer

I love to drink
therefore
steps must be taken
small
      ones
           sipped

like this tot of Glenlivet
good for an hour
a single malt right
           enough.

MY NEW PAD

In your tall white A4 pages
I'll write A1 poems that go
On and on and on right to the
Bottom a frigid foot away
Beneath your plain brown wrapper
I shall be fanciful: foul mouthed or
Exemplary as Zwingli You're the
Tablet I'm taking, the snow I
Plough. Now the long lean poems
Will abseil down your steep
White cliff if I'm given enough
Old rope. Before the *Muji* pad
I turned over dry new leaves
Or filled wee notebooks with bowed,
Slope shouldered, stunted verses.
O my poems! Stretch,
Breathe, jump, run; be natural
Clear and dauntless
Snow melt on Mt Fuji.

GRACE BEFORE MEALS

Such savour in an apple
a hunk or two of bread
a mouse's morsel of French
                    fromage
maybe on a high day
a cup or so of soup
wine certainly
one round red glass
and music *moderato*
in these good lean times.

MOTORING

Nobody in Italy grows up wanting
to be a train driver

Nobody anywhere wants to grow up

Nobody knows the car ads I've seen
Nobody knows but Jesus
I'd like a new Fiat Ego
In egg yolk yellow or brain haemorrhage red
CD included zero per cent interest
going from handbrake to blazes
In the time it takes to wind down
the window and shout *waaaaanker!*
Fuck them with their asthma
I'm *fuming* (have you tried the choke)
Look you're the bloke that broke
down so get it off the road pronto
I can afford a Ford but I'd rather
have a BMW getting paid
and laid accordingly. Keeping a
sun roof over my head!
Your car's your character Your character's your car
know what I mean
Eco cosy, windscreen tinted really rosy
punningly named cunningly aimed
at your willie and your wallet
What can you say O
try My God (or better yet) *Mon Deo* . . .

PENANG

Barrelling along
in the blustery drizzle of December
with Richard (for once)
that quarter pace behind
I'm in love again with Glasgow
and my squat square mile
of the wild West End.

I'm by Picasso
massy and round

but Giacometti made Richard
who
might
blow
away

Such fancies are fine
in the run up to Christmas
with the 'Mata Hari'
just a brisk step away
due East on West
                    Princes
in the car alarmed night

Alluring as always
the satay is tender
our noodles and fish
mysteriously spiced
coconut and ginger
an espionage of coriander
winey secrets, code word
'Medoc' which may not be
Malaysian but is warming and cheap
and goes well with chopsticks
and the torrid palette
of Hock aun Teh
whose sun struck abstracts

giggle on the walls.
In season
oriental song birds
                    chit chat
on the terrace but tonight
winter holds a finger to its lips
and we dine a deux, alone
Our waitress
is taking her finals
at Glasgow
In electrical engineering
but plans to go back

In the meantime she slips us clues
in the Tourist Board 'promotion'
There are fabulous prizes . . .
so Mata Hari means 'rising sun'
Richard and I sip claret
licking garlic off sealed lips
planning our exploits
on the lam in Penang

GREAT WESTERN ROAD

Glasgow, you look beatific in blue
and I've a Saturday before me
for galleries and poems,
a house full of Haydn,
and beneath my kitchen window,
tennis stars in saris
lobbing backhands at the bins.
French coffee, and who knows maybe
Allen Ginsberg in my bath!
then round to the dairy
where scones are cooling on the rack
and Jimmy won't let me leave
till I've tried one there and then,
here, where the new Glasgow started –
an old grey city going blonde

whose Asian shops are full of fruits
we owe to Cap'n Bligh
and I'm so juiced I could walk clear
to Loch Lomond,
past buses stripping the willow
all along Great Western Road
but I just browse bargains in banjos
and pop-art knitted ties,
before checking out the crime section
at Caledonia Books
finding friesias in the flowershops
and in the second hand record store,
Bruckner's Third,
The Cleveland
under Szell:
so sad; like falling for passing students
with that black haired, blue eyed look,
or buying basil and chorizos . . .
In the afternoon I'll look at paintings
in Dougie Thomson's Mayfest show,
maybe stroll down to the studio
to view some archive film,
past the motorways and multi-storeys
of Grieve's Ultimate Cowcaddens
the peeling pawn at George's Cross
where, today, everything is redeemable
because tonight there'll be guitar poets
from Russia at the Third Eye Centre.
And later I'll cook zarzuela
for a new and nimble friend.
God Glasgow it's glorious
just to gulp you down in heartfuls,
feeling something quite like love.

3
Marche Funèbre

MARCHE FUNEBRE

I

When they called me to the phone
in the STV canteen I didn't guess.
Just work. The usual Yes,
I could be ready in ten minutes
then again not in ten years.
Maureen. Mum. Then I knew
with the hospital again so soon
That it was serious. On the
motorway keeping cheerful
already it seemed too late
A raw white morning. Colder
in the heated car

II

Gone just minutes before.
The news from a woman doctor
Maureen's age twenty-six or so?
Peacefully in her sleep Those
very words; that *phrase*
Maureen's quiet quaking sobs
Me too busy 'mastering' myself
To reach out to her
until the stethoscoped stranger did
Then a bare hug dry eyed and ashamed
You can see her if you'd like.

IV

The only tears I ever saw
my father shed
I witnessed when I told him she was dead
Only sixty and he turned eighty-one
Is she dead Donny
Is she really dead son
Him by the hearth
Me in Hester's place
No No No No No No sputtered like
a propeller till it formed one moan,
Our first and last embrace

V

Tapas and Rioja near the Kelvin Hall
Another first; Stephen and me drunk
I'm the boozy maudlin one
but tonight Sergeant O'Rourke
let's R.I.P. Though we are flushed
and sentimental we are not teary
We laugh until it doesn't hurt
The model cum weathergirl
and her highlit friends at
the next table are infected
and smile crocodiley along. Anyone
would think we had something
to celebrate. *Anyone would be*
dead right.

VI

In the church the heater
did its dinger, an oil
guffy giggle
every minute or two.
Mary the priest called you, Mother
of Christ, *Mary* that's a
laugh, when to all and sundry
(except on Sunday) you were
Hester though only for a lifetime or so!
Verbal enbalming fluid, off the
peg unction, not one customised
word for our 'dear departed sister
Mary'! 'Fuck this' I want
to bawl and bowl up
to the altar, extempore
specific *memories* foaming on my
lips. Not even your
Christian name's alive mother.

On eight stout shoulders we
largoed you down the aisle

VII

On the coldest day
of that or any other year,

your sons helped
lower you tenderly away

into hard black clay
so cold it had to be dug

mechanically. No surgeon
cut the cords this time

we meekly let them go —
two grieving brothers

grown to look a little bit
like you, neither one able to

grasp any longer
what it feels like

to go home.

VIII

The parish priest
was pious and impersonal but
blessedly short winded in deference
to the snow.

Apart from his overboiled greens
and purples and the quiet riot
of the wreaths we didn't want,
all colour had been obliterated
by three days of arctic drifts

our loss not yet subtle
still reeling on

in terse black and white

IX

Mum the Bishopton Hotel
was booked up and pricey

no better now than on your
only visit a score of years

ago; so Maureen (God Bless
her) hit upon 'Formakin'

The 'Monkey House' of yore
not half a mile from here

slow ambled goal of many's
the summer stroll for

Maureen and Stephen and me
you and Dad bringing up

the rear. Pickard's place
a cinema magnate's folly

Edwardian throwback to
the House of Usherette
pile paid for
from pile made
at Greens Playhouse
the eponymous chizzled chimps
crouching on the wall.

X

Mother darling, shock haired
and heavy, I am so your son!

too fat of late to fit
my only suit. Under the

navy Loden I wore
an ancient loose black

cardigan you never
would have given your

obiter dicta acht well Good taste
as opposed to *form*
was aye my strong suit
Donny boy, You look powerfully like Frank

was the candid consensus
And I am as dark and ruddy

as your beefy bristle browed brother,
the well read uncle I

always took after, the mentor
who loaned me Fitzgerald

and O'Hara, till he said
with a sigh sure it's a *poet* you are

Maître d' of baked meats and whisky
I've supplanted my father in the

rigmarole of grief. I've the
right word for everybody

under the circumstances

a mother lost: the common
touch attained.

XI
I never thought until today that where you lie's
like Antrim: soft green, *growing* land
under all that snow.
The mountains of Argyll though,
on the other side this time. Our only bad blood
was mopped up in my teens all five of us close;
unfashionably fond. No idyll. Not ideal
but real

love all the same.
When I came
home at Christmas and went nostalgically
to mass you waited up for me
the way you did for years. Twisting your arm
as I twisted the cork out of the claret I
remembered bed time drinks in that first
quiet house. You weren't a drinker mother, but
we sipped and talked for hours. Although I'd no
morbid 'premonition' still I marked that deep accord
It snowed then too.
But lightly

XII
Duty done I take a wee turn round the grounds.
We fished here, feared the gamekeeper's gun:
Now they take my cheque, do a very decent scone,
Keep straight faces for the funerals but have
winning wedding smiles no doubt. Soon Dad will rest
here too. That's not bad taste: just timing and statistics.
They swore to share a layer. In weather
worse than this when he was a boy, Dan
rooted for turnips near the Kilmacolm Road
not poor merely but *starving*, unwilling to give in
Now his will's all weariness and grief
as he leafs through the papers in the foyer,
A blizzard between him and Bishopton
BRITAIN CANCELLED — was the headline in the Sun.

I.M. M.H. Quigg: 1930–1991
requiescat in pace

4

An Early Bath

'Wantoness for ever mair
Wantoness has been my ruin
Yet for all my doul and care
It's wantoness for ever'.

Robert Burns, '*Wantoness*'

'Of course we should dream of all women. There isn't one of them who wouldn't be offended if a man didn't dream of all of them through her.'

Jean Baudrillard, *Cool Memories*

STEPPING OUT

It's me, It's Saturday
I've got nothing on
(I just stepped out the
bath so pardon the pun)
It's oh what yeah a smidgeon
after three
If there's no-one special
why not spend tonight with me
I could shake you up
a cocktail at seven or so
What do you reckon let me know
I'll serve some monkfish
in a saffron sauce
There's tarragon for the
salad which you can toss
with some extra virgin oil
Just like you used to –
Provençal style
while I'm footering
in the kitchen I'll leave the Blue Nile
to explain Glasgow to
you. Miles
Davis' *Birth of the
Cool* (*Darn That Dream*)
Remember? will spool
anachronistically on cassette
But I won't forget
That we're just friends
There's a Gewurtztraminer
here that will make amends
That's all
So call?

LIKE SIMONE SIGNORET

Perhaps it was the weather
Wet and hot
Or the poems of Prévert
She'd just bought
Watching her browse
I decided now's
the time to make a play
But I just let it pelt
while she knotted her belt
like Simone Signoret.

When she asked the quickest way
To Buchanan Street
I suggested coffee
If she'd no-one to meet
Sharing her umbrella
I was that Montand fella
Très distingué
A boulevard romance
A Glasgow Saturday in France
with Simone Signoret

Sartre's making speeches
in George's Square
The scent of wine and garlic
in the air.
Freedom too.
It reminds you
of '68: and May
Paving stones; Sûreté citroens
And Simone Signoret

She'd bought the poems for a friend
Didn't read that much
Though in the café our heads were close,
They didn't touch.
Waving her goodbye
I wonder why

I'm still a fool this way
A look over her shoulder
That self-sufficient smoulder
Simone Signoret

FOLLOW

Sufficient and justified
on Cathedral Street
In the rain

                    we feed
each other chips
letting John Knox
show us the way
to go
home

                    Going west
at his behest
the Tron's wersh wine
                    vinegary
on our tongues

ok so taxis tip us
their tangerine winks
we are tired
                    it is late

but darling if you will only run
we can catch that green and yellow bus
yes, change is essential
but we have it in handsful

There's sambucca
                    on the sideboard
Piazzolla will play for us.

I'll lay out the tango cloth
we can follow the footsteps
on my hard yellow floor.

HOME AND AWAY

After an extra week away
I come home to carnations
spoiling in their vase
and one bad apple
trying to shed its skin
Your note is on the window
sill, curling slightly
in the late December damp.

SOME CONSOLATION

So we were only a fling
and not the grand amour you long
for. Now you're playing John Field's nocturnes
late into the night, hob nobbing
entre nous and *heart to heart*
pouring out vino like some sob story,
calling old flames at God knows
what hour and me foul names, you
who have broken good men's hearts

as casually as midweek high school dates,
you who revel in all this love lorn
drapes drawn palaver, driving til dawn
to hurl Rilke across the *'perfect'* estuary

Be grateful. We lasted longer than a petrol
station rose and now you're blue
as it could never be.

WINE AND WOOING

I wasn't the first one
I wasn't the worst one
You called me your baleful boy
After all the losers
And cynical users
There was no cause to be coy
So what you wanted you named and took
And the name you chose was mine
Yours was the first grown woman's look
That I knew to be love's sign

You taught me wine and wooing
I learned by candlelight
To do what needed doing
To do it slow, and right?

It was your proud prime
And my first time
You wept but wouldn't say
What joys or fears
Had caused the tears
As the dark spring night turned grey —
Again that look, but what you took
Was your loving leave of me
The callow shallow lad mistook
How a woman's heart comes free

You taught me wine and wooing
I learned by candlelight
To do what needed doing
To do it slow, and right?

On other nights
When brighter lights
Glow in younger eyes
Older now and bolder now
Still waiting to be wise
All I know and show of love
was learned that night we shared
Long ago in Glasgow
When you looked at me and dared.

NAW, LUVE ISNAE DEID

Frae thi French o Robert Desnos

Naw, luve isnae deid in this hert an these een an this mou
    that
scryed thi fore-end o its ain requiem.
    Tak tent, Ah've hud eneugh o thi picteresque, o colours an
        chairm
    Ah *luv* luv, its frushness an ill kinditness.
    Thi wan Ah luv hiz ae yin nem, a singil furm.
    A things gang. Mous clap til this mou.
    Thi wan Ah luv, hiz jeest wan nem, wan furm.
    And somewhiles gin ye min it
    O Ye, furm an nem o ma luv,
    Wan day oan thi main atween Americay an Europe,
    Whan thi lest leam o sunlicht skinkles ower thi scruif o thi
        kelterin swaw,
Or ense wan roilin nicht ablow a birk in thi kintra, or hail tear
    in a motor,
    Wan voar day morn Woodlands Road,
    Wan blashie day,
    At skreich o daw, afore pittin yersel tae bed,
    Clash yersel, ah hoy yer weel kent ghaist, that ah wiz thi ae
        wan tae loo
ye mair an whit a sin ye nivvir kent it.
    Clash yersel ye maun no be vext fur oniethin: afore me
        Ronsard an Baude-
laire chauntit thi dools o auld wummin an deid yins wha

miscawed thi purest luv.
ye, whan ye dee,
Ye will be bonny an glaggered fur yet.
Ah'll be deid lang syne areddies, whately fauldit in yer immortal
lyke, in yer
dumfounerrin parrymauk fur aye present amang thi nivvir
upplin wunners o lif an
thi ivvirlastin but gin Ah ootlast ye
Yon vyce o yours an hoo it souns, yer glower an hoo it
glents,
thi smeek o ye an yer dabberlacks an monie anither hing'll
still

gang oan

livin in me.

In me an Ah'm nae Ronsard or Baudelaire,
Jist me Robert Desnos wha, fur haen kent ye an looed ye,
Is as guid as they ur,
Jist me Robert Desnos wha, fur looin ye
Disnae want tae be mindit fur oniethin ense oan this
sneistsome
scruiffin.

MAIREAD IN THE MIRROR

Mairead in the mirror
Is a sight for sore eyes
She smiles at her smile
And to her surprise
Says beautiful you're beautiful
And wise

Mairead in the mirror
Tries a strawberry pout
He didn't call
But she's going out
She'll paint her nails and the town, red, without

73

The guy who keeps her by the telephone
On Saturday for hours
Who buys her budget bouquets
Of her most detested flowers
Who orders sweet vermouth
When she'd sooner whisky sours
Who when he meets male friends of hers
Sulks, silently and glowers
Who always says 'mine' not 'ours'
One of those empty house rowers
With Warren Beattie's powers
(He thinks).

Mairead in the mirror is talking tough.
She'll call a cab, call his bluff
He's had his chance
She's had enough.

Mairead in the mirror is
Looking strong
Putting on her make-up
To a Streisand song
She can see herself
And be herself
It's been too long

Mairead in the mirror
Is a sight for sore eyes
She smiles at her smile
And to her surprise
Says beautiful you're beautiful
And wise.

AN EARLY BATH

To prove, I think, despite all evidence
That last night, our first night
Was no mistake, you draw a bath for us
In the warm first light of this citrus sharp
Spring morning. You wash my hair, oil
My joints with a slow erotic thoroughness –

All this to the sound of Mozart clarinets.

With the tang of your keen kisses
Still sudsy on my lips,
I embrace anew the end in these beginnings

That leave me perfumed and anointed, barely salved . . .

While I brew coffee you soak blithely on
Ticking off on spotless toes the splashy plans
That count me safely in. Dear Geisha,

I'll towel you now, but who will dry your tears?

I have never been so clean or felt so dirty.

GOLD

Through a wine glass today in a Soho bistro
I saw you dear ghost of 1979.
Micro skirt and air wear shoes, those red
Framed specs that telly people pick
To filter histories out. You were with a louche
And deferential, slightly younger man.
Watching you trump his Amex Gold
With your own glistering plastic
I thought of nights in the city of Glasgow
When all the gold you wanted
Was the light of my open door.

RESORT

Long before I butterfingered your lucky heirloom tumbler
we were more or less washed up but that night

the warning light definitely came on while we panned
and shovelled shards of leaded Irish crystal

in the scullery cum kitchenette of the coup
you'd rented to be closer. Clammy nights

of fervent, futile, fucking, our cum cries ever
more lunatically raucous until both of us

were barking. Our brave faces deserved medals.
We grinned but couldn't bear it, still tried

gamely one more time, what the hell, a doughty
short lived stab at couples in a heat wavering

Welsh resort at the fullest top-most tip
of what ought to have been our season. You were

perfect then, I priapic in my prime that peachy
last weekend, two, too hot days between ripe and rotten.

LAMMAS (for J. S.)

Autumn puts the gust in August
The wind smells of stale pale ale
The castle goes up in firework smoke
Mine's a double in this RLS tale

Another summer's over
The curtains all come down
Its a Festivalediction
For an old souled town

When the calendar's done its wilkies

76

I'll be back in Charlotte Square
And you'll be where your dreams go next
While I think of you and drink to you, there

In the closes of the old town
I'll make the cobbles ring
With Ramsay Burns and Fergusson
and the songs you bade me sing
And your other half
will chase and quaff
Caol Ila ordered with
a glass of 80 shilling
and the ghost of Goodsir Smith.

When the calendar's done its wilkies
I'll be back in Charlotte Square
And you'll be where your dreams go next
While I think of you and drink to you, there

IN THE ELEVENTH MONTH

Today the light's like tablet
on the sandstone and every shrub's
a burning bush. Wind wizened elms
play peek a boo with a winter sky
so blamelessly blue a Florentine Fra
would think his palette blessed
with just a luscious dab or two

The hills beyond Maryhill
show off their shiny new November
quilt; I bend gladly over my morning
work at a wide window facing North
a tall pile of beloved books at one elbow smoky bitter
tea at the other. My love lives many
miles beyond the snowy mountains

No missive from me would be welcome

ADULTS IN THE DARK

She waved me to the window
Said look at all the rain
You can't go out in that that's flat
So I sat back down again
Chet Baker started singing
Stella by Starlight
Only the wine was breathing
Be a friend, please spend the night.

A Hyndland Sunday morning
Radio and rolls
The aftermath of a playpool bath
Ricicles in bowls
A little kid stuff kidding
We were adults in the dark
At what was said half drunk in bed
You're crying in the park.

Coupledom defeats us but we're scared to live alone
Children still until fulfilled, by children of our own
Yet rather than commitment we commit the same old crime
Flirty us at thirty plus
Hoping this time
Maybe this will be the big one
Ensemble en famille
No hit and run no passing fun
Us instead of me
Not just making love and taking love
But giving love at last
There's been so much faking love
Living out my past.

SILKIE (For M.B.)

It'll be light still in mild Tiree,
The water warm enough for swimming.
My window's up but no spray brines
The air on Woodlands Road.
The poems you left are read:
Later I'll dedicate a tall green candle to them.
Now I drink wine, play a harp tune on the guitar,
It is, *Tamdair dom do lamh* – Give me your hand –

Bask soon dear Silkie
In the blue bays of my heart.

ROCKS

I

Tonight darling the blues blew in
And I'm listless and mopey without you
You're in 'my' hotel in San Francisco –
Happy the card says, *perfectly*
I'm halfway through the new Philip Kerr
Farther through the wine, wishing Stephen
was a little closer than the Sussex Coast
And that Maureen had fewer worries of her own –
That our parents were still just a phone
call away. Dad's three years dead, Mum four.
I miss them less often but more
when I do and I do now terribly.
Between me and wherever they are
There's a void I avoid with
late nights and liquor
certain records our whole family enjoyed
and yes, one or two of 'our' songs –
You know the ones

II

On Feast Days in Dowanhill you'd feed me
Fare Breton your pruney egg nog

Coup de grace. I'm all chunky intuition —
And so loved the delicacies you sliced and diced

From cookbooks and colour-supplement recipes
That used no meat. Such finesse. Yes

I miss those limey G and Ts slurped with pistachios
On your tiny balcony that seemed so *Parisienne*

Van Morrison? Mel Torme? I never play
them without missing you a little, never

use recipes at all

III

Jo did you really never know
That your name in Scots means *darling*
In the cottage at Anstruther
I would sing you *My Pittenweem Jo*,
And that you were. Like John Anderson
Or the term Burns preferred to 'dear'
In the original version of *Auld Lang Syne*.

IV

Islay love. Weren't we happy on *Islay*?
Halving the laundry bill in our big yellow
Well lit, twin-bedded room, overlooking the
Distillery and the harbour at Bowmore
No more tranquil bolt-hole could be conjured
The still summer evenings, mellow with malt
In the mauve to magenta late gloamings of June.
Between us and Colonsay, on the blowy West side,
More sorts of seabird than I'd ever seen
Even without the binoculars you'd forgotten
On Islay our normal sized life seemed suddenly sufficient
Full scale, like the Celtic cross at Kildonan

80

Blown up from the replica on my desk
Seals slithered in the seawood
At Lagavulin Bay, yelping in the dulse
That lends that dram its peaty, iodine reek.
On the creamy sill of my kitchen window
Twelve pale pebbles, bobble in a bowl.
You have your own stone pot pourri
To jiggle calmly in the palm that
Lay in my free hand the afternoon we
Stooped to comb the beach, each choosing
For the other, these grey green precious stones
I call my Islay blues

DURING THE BEEP (for X, Y and Z)

When I play the message back
Your voice is moist
With tears and a drop or two
Too much: the Chardonnay
Just calling to say
That there's this film I ought to see,
Now you're all over me
A pally G and T
For old times sake . . .

A pause and then
'After the beep you creep,
I know you're home and still awake
Let's speak midweek, it's naff
To screen your calls',
You laugh
Scolding me in your cups
As I pad back to bed
And the medical student
I was busy picking up.

HIGHER ORDINARY

From the sixth floor of the University Library Glasgow can be seen going about what's left of its business while we go about ours – scraping thirds in a modern language or mentally subtracting minuses from a drop dead Alpha essay sure to set the Spenser and numerology seminar rocking on its (fourteen!) heels. Most of us are Higher Ordinary.

The giveaway's the way they take notes with the no flies nonchalance of Hunter S Thompson *and* the editorial discrimination of a court stenographer on piece work, scowling sardonically then regressing, going all overawed and smiley. Junior Honours footer with their haircuts like conditioner ad hopefuls, experts in denim 'quotes' and sexy sitting, offering the example of their prodigious profiles to lecturers and freshers alike. Half glances twinkle in the twilight.

Boy meets girl: girl gets giggles: girl gets boy. Get this! The entire floor is heaving with hormones. Thank God and Le Corbusier this isn't the shoogly shockable old Bodleian but a fine upstanding sixties concrete tower block with the peerless vistas I already mentioned and a November sunset I didn't, like a continuous curl of orange peel beyond the violet river and the smoky hills. Mauve ices Gilbert Scott's doomsday cake confection. Looks like lilac goes with Govan and the drouthy drooping cranes. In the livid livery of hacked off Strathclyde, a sprinter train huffs East.

It's so gemütlich up here they should rotate Level Six 360°, install a cocktail lounge, pipe in a little low key jazz, some cool and mellow Miles or maybe Chet Baker (no, *that* notion is out the window, given poor Chet's track record on trips and trajectory) but Billie Holiday – whoever. Anyhow, then we could do the hair thing, the precision slouching, go for long, willowy, interdisciplinary walks, sneek shuftis through the shelving in that shadowy stretch all the way from Shakespeare to Bernard Shaw, read books sometimes even, if we had a mind to, all the while highballing each other over ice cubes and liquor way up on 'Cloud Six'. The senate could franchise the entire operation. A nice wee concession for the right fund-holding student.

But I shouldn't joke; I've spent a perfect afternoon with unconscionable James Dickey. And when this joint closes Ann Sexton's coming home with me.

BEAT

All he needs for a lifelong trip
Is the change of clothing in his old tan grip
A notebook full of poems with bedroom eyes
To charm a new true love wherever he lies

He's on the road and the beat goes on
The seeds Jack sowed, the wheat grows on
He's a Dharma Bum. Got the Mexico Blues
Let the Karma come with the grass and booze

He's next in line to be the next big thing
In a vision Jim crowned him Lizard King
He's got Ginsberg and Corso off by heart
His art's his life — his life's his art

He's on the road and the beat goes on
The seeds Jack sowed, the wheat grows on
He's a Dharma Bum. Got the Mexico Blues
Let the Karma come with the grass and booze

Alex Trocchi came to Partick in a mushroom cloud
Muttering a mantra but the crowd was too loud
At the all day **poetryon** *at Ibrox park*
Where generation Xstacy was whistling in the dark

He's on the road and the beat goes on
The seeds Jack sowed, the wheat grows on
He's a Dharma Bum. Got the Mexico Blues
Let the Karma come with the grass and booze

INDIGO AND ORANGE

Irises and lilies —
Still her favourite flowers
Withering in the window
Like my fading powers
Indigo and orange
A vase of lacquered black
A Japanese reminder
She's not coming back

And it's bad but getting better
Yes it's sad but I'll forget her
Just like she put me out of mind
Wherever she is now
And with whom
I won't allow
Any thoughts that are not kind.

The radio spills Scriabin
Like a drunken lover's tears
And I'm pouring the first coffee
I have drunk alone in years

And it's bad but getting better
Yes it's sad but I'll forget her
Just like she put me out of mind
Wherever she is now
And with whom
I won't allow
Any thoughts that are not kind.

And there's rock salt on the pavements
And more snow on the way
And I'm slipping into wondering
Why she couldn't stay.

And it's bad but getting better
Yes it's sad but I'll forget her
Just like she put me out of mind

84

Wherever she is now
And with whom
I won't allow
Any thoughts that are not kind.

DR POETRY

Eh hello
        is that

            Dr Poetry

Yes, poet, identify yourself.

Em, this is Donny O'Rourke
or actually Daniel sometimes
confusingly

in-de-cision, Donny/Dan
not good. Your problem?

Yes. I published a small volume
in 1991 called Second Cities
Simon Armitage gave it an excellent review
and it was a Glasgow Herald
'critic's choice' for that year.
It's now out of print and I've published virtually nothing since
Can you help me?
I think I might be an ex poet . . .

Donny/Dan you're ALL poet
nothing BUT poet.
You will write again. Soon. TONIGHT *. . .*
I need to know two things
where you at

and your credit card number.